Spiritual Writers Network

Presents

Illuminations of the Soul

A Poetry Anthology

Spiritual Writers Network

Presents

Illuminations of the Soul

A Poetry Anthology

ISBN-13: 978-0692524411
ISBN-10: 069252441X

Printed in the United States of America

"*Owning our story can be hard but not nearly as difficult as spending our lives running from it. Embracing our vulnerabilities is risky but not nearly as dangerous as giving up on love and belonging and joy—the experiences that make us the most vulnerable. Only when we are brave enough to explore the darkness will we discover the infinite power of our light.*"

~ Brené Brown

CONTENTS

1ˢᵗ Place Winner

Reflections on a Passing

by R.D. Petti

I am the current running,
In dark watery depths,
Bringing life in perpetual motion.

I am ripples made from a breeze
Softly dancing on my surface,
Playing host to lily pads and reeds,
And squawking geese.

I am glassy stillness,
Mirroring puffs of clouds above,
Tree boughs overhanging, and
A white crane flying low
With outstretched wings.

I am the reflection
Of the moon and starry skies,
Of dreams and souls.

I am the astral tryst
For lovers of 63 years,
One in spirit, the other left behind,
Swimming with abandon,
In my healing waters.

I am the crossroads,
Welcoming the other,
Who stands at my water's edge,
As her lover beckons to her
To swim with him once again.

I am peace for their daughter,
Who sits on my bank
In silent, loving reverence of
Their rich earthly sojourn,
And the gifts they unconditionally
Gave to her and to all who
Were fortunate to cross their paths.

I am serenity,
I am radiance,
I am vibrancy,
I am life eternal.

Ash Wednesday, 2012
Mother's Cremation Day

R.D. Petti is a mystic, poet, and debut author of the spiritual fantasy Nettie's Tea House: A Tale of the Afterlife. Having earned a B.A. in English Literature and M.A. in Counseling Psychology, she has been a life-long student of consciousness, seeking knowledge and wisdom found in mystery and spiritual traditions. With a background in mental health counseling and hospice, she delved into the field of death and dying during her parents' transitions. Through her dreamtime experiences, she has become passionate in her desire to bring this miraculous passage to light as well as the wonder-filled world of spirit. She currently resides in Sarasota, Florida.

2ⁿᵈ Place Winner

The Woe of My Color

by Debra Chimuka

Why am I estranged?
    Who has words to describe color?
Who has words to define man?
What meanest thou my skin?
Causing me woe and tears.

    Alas thou art something to think about!
If you are so cruel;
To take my sense of self.
Who decides who qualifies for this color?
Who is the judge?

    None chose to be pitch black like baboons
    Nor pink like pigs.
Judging and criticizing;
And being judged and criticized
The root of separatism.

    My color at the back of the class
This black unprivileged shade;
Chained to my color, I change not
My skin cannot be from me nor I.

    There are no words to express
The feelings that overwhelm me when I am;
Degraded, patronized and profiled because of my color.
No! Don't touch me!
Anger and pain combined:

    The pain shuts off my words;
My breathing is shallow and tense;

The weight of pain is heavy;
Resentment rocks my senses and body.

Without ways to fight back;
You cut me deeper than any knife could ever do
I bled where you could not see.
I bled within;
There was no blood but pain.
Your words and conduct cutting me into parts
Until there was no me---but only you.

My color is not stupidity;
Only my actions can be.
Beneath my skin
Is the key to finding me!
Every color scheme is beauty through;
Pure insight.

Once you associate habits with color
Labels and habits interfere with true identity.
My color is not a defect,
A fair character, the real meaning of a human being
That alone makes one superior.

When one who is racially biased dies or falls to the
ground;
Prejudicial thoughts are buried with him.
The shutter is closed
No more racial bullying
Spite cannot touch me anymore.
This is my freedom and his bliss;
As he lies down resting in non-contending peace.

3rd Place Winner

The Pearl

by Megan Moffitt

My mother gave me a name, and it meant "pearl,"

A gem of silent, understated beauty,

A precious secret behind a curtain of shyness.

Other jewels stood out more boldly against the black velvet backdrop-

Hard, sharp, bright girls like diamonds,

Ruby girls like cold burning fires,

Serene emerald girls-

But I was always the pearl.

The pearl is lonely yet patient,

Always trusting that one day she will be found.

The pearl is quiet but watchful,

Gazing deep into the hearts of men

Too blind to see their own reflections.

I, the pearl, am love and white light,

Enduring calm and hope.

The wisdom cradled in the dragon's claw,

The treasure for which the oyster must die.

I am fragile and imperfect,

But a gift from the primordial sea,

Honest and true.

I am a promise and a wish,

Tender as a mermaid's kiss.

Megan Moffitt is a visually impaired writer from Northern California. She currently attends classes at her local community college, where her favorite subject, as it has always been in school, is English. After earning her general education credits, she plans to transfer to a state university, where she will study journalism. Her dream is to one day work with bands, combining her passion for words with her love of music by conducting interviews, writing album reviews, and promoting via social media. During her high school years, Megan had several poems printed in her school's literary magazine, and she worked as a columnist for her city's newspaper in 2012. Besides being a poet and short story author, she is a certified Reiki master, member of a Buddhist meditation group, animal lover, peace advocate, and indie rock fan. She is most deeply inspired by the smoke-scented autumn wind, the sound of the ocean, random acts of kindness, the movie Rent, and the novel The Perks of Being a Wallflower.

Millions of Reasons to Smile Today

by Louise Huey Greenleaf

As we waken this morning
let us mindfully pray,
for some millions of reasons
to smile today.

An abundant buffet
clad from heaven above,
overflowing and bursting
with God's holy love

For each leaf on each tree
may all count as one,
every bird that flies by
and the warmth of the sun.

To each whom we meet
let us greet with a smile,
take a peek at the clouds
even just for a while.

Vision strawberries, butterflies, prayers,
children laughing. Rainbows, puppies,
and flowers in bloom. Poetry, music,
elderly wisdom, a stroll in the park
in the cool afternoon.

All wondrous gifts
like the coo of a dove,
just as *everyone's* smile
is laced with God's love

Then when the day ends

let our memories portray,
all those millions of reasons
we smiled today.

It seems more and more evident that our lives have become beyond busy these days. We have become so jam-packed with endless responsibilities, and exorbitant activities, that we're losing touch with taking even just a *snippet* of time to relax our minds, and nourish our souls with the simple and abundant gifts that are *everywhere* around us. Take in, and enjoy!

I am a 35 year survivor of Multiple Sclerosis. Though having been permanently confined to a wheelchair since 2 004, I embrace my physical challenges through my faith in Jesus Christ, and celebrate the stillness in my life by sharing my stories and poems which are published through Spiritual Writers Network//Transcendent Publishing. For further information I may be contacted at louisehgreenleaf@gmail.com T go to sleep Thank you for your interest.

Silent Study

by Edda Fretz

I sit silently in
a room of silence.
The walls are silently
screaming at me.

Nature is winking silently
through the window, beckoning me
to come out and play.

I sit waiting with the silent
fire engine red telephone.
Waiting for that shrilly ringing
sound to burst this bubble of silence.

Thoughts silently drift through
my mind, causing echo's in my heart.
Images float silently through the
visual hemisphere to be scrutinized.

The silence is deafening.
The wind rustles the leaves,
teasing me to participate,
outside this soundproof wall of glass.

I meditate and visualize rainbow
colors of light, slipping around me as a
silent glow, radiating out and to others.
Those who in their silence are open,

to receive what they need.

Bathing in the Universe's unspoken language,
I continue to sit centered in silence.
A peacefulness settles over me and
the realization that silence is an important
part of you, quietly slips in embracing me.

My Inspiration

by Jacquie Lamica

Like sitting upon a wild ride taking in all that meets your
senses.
The fresh breath of a new spring day and the awakening of
something new.
Like a dawn the sun arises, your face captivates me like the
hummingbird
suckling the nectar of a flower giving me life and reason to
fly.
Like a gentle rain I feel refreshed, fulfilled to meet new
challenges
As if the rainbow began and ended with the smile reflected
in your eyes.
Like a novel filled with mysteries, I turn the pages to each
new chapter.
Encountering and experiencing so many new feelings
Life is a journey and as I turn the corner, it's you that I
have traveled with.
I have spent so much of my life with you looking for
happiness.
Could it have been you, my inspiration?

*Jacquie Lamica is a freelance writer who loves to put words to her
experiences and dreams thru poetry. "Wears her heart on her sleeve"
has been used all too often to describe her.*

*Jacquie has a Bachelors degree in Psychology and is currently studying
to get her credentials in the field of Alzheimers/Dementia. She is a
full-time caregiver for her aging mother who has this same devastating
disease.*

She loves to try new recipes in the kitchen and also creates unique crocheted accessories.

Jacquie lives in the serene wine country of Sonoma County in Northern California.

Resurrection

by Sibyl Dana Reynolds

Perhaps deep in a cave
or beneath a mossy stone
or hidden in an abandoned desk inside a secret cupboard
or a splintered forgotten drawer
there is a tattered remnant
carefully folded
like a star
exactly as it was folded by the alchemist
who recorded on the now ancient square of parchment,
the recipe for an elixir that when
stirred with the index finger and sipped slowly
while watching the moon slowly rise in the mid-winter sky
cures cancer
and AIDS
and makes angels of demons
and goodness from evil
and hope from despair.

Sibyl is the award-winning author of the novel, Ink and Honey, and the soon to be released companion guidebook, The Way of Belle Cœur: A Woman's Vade Mecum. She is a spiritual director and the founder of the new monastic community, the Sisterhood of Belle Cœur. Passionate about the value of the teachings of the medieval Christian mystics, sacred art making, and the power of women's stories, Sibyl draws inspiration from these forms of spiritual and creative wisdom to inform her writing and work. Her website SacredLifeArts.com is an online sanctuary, classroom and resource center dedicated to bringing creative inspiration and spiritual illumination to women. Sibyl also served as the first Roman Catholic Woman Bishop of North America (Roman Catholic Women Priests), now retired. For additional information about Sibyl and her work you may visit her websites: InkandHoneytheBook.com and SacredLifeArts.com. She will have a new website in 2016, SibylDanaReynolds.com.

Muddy Waters

by Chaya Rosen

Did you really think
you could keep me here
in the folds of your words
where your world holds
a cover to hide inside fear

Full disclosure deceit seeps
sweeps over line surfaces
that separate and fragment
hardened like mortar
seal into pores

Soles sink below your feet
stand naked in the rubble
foot prints absorb
your screams and schemes
your slaughter your murder

I'll spread my wings
upon you
coronate each letter
with a brush of truth
until this bloody muddy earth
ceases to sink beneath its own dirge

Chaya Rosen's multi-cultural background includes an upbringing heavily influenced by a strong spiritual framework in Israel, as a daughter of Holocaust survivors. She received a BA in Communication from the University of Colorado and a Masters of Science in Management from Rivier College, New Hampshire.

Her writing is based on a lifelong introspective quest, coming to terms with healing, recovery and repair. Her published works include three poetry books: Streaming Light, Scattered Stones, and the newly released:
In the Shadow of God.

In My Time of Dismay

by Stephanie Uelese Jackson

They plot; they plan; they wonder about
I feel like David in his time of despair
I sit and stare wondering if I should care
Some days are more than I can bare
They plot, they plan, they wonder about
I see their traps in my path
Like King Solomon I pray for wisdom
I look for her to show me a way
Especially during this time of dismay
My heart cries out in utter disbelief
While my soul searches for some kind of relief
They plot; they plan; they wonder about
I look to my faith to keep me safe
I'm on my knees praying to thee
Keep me within his mercy and grace
Like a child in distress
I find refuge within my father
My heart that is filled with heartache and anguish
He welcomes his daughter with love and adoration
He wipes away her tears of frustration
And replaces them with joy and manifestation
They plot; they plan; they wonder about
When all else has failed I look
To the words of my brother Paul
"Finally, my brothers and sisters, always think about what
is true.
Think about what is noble, right and pure.
Think about what is lovely and worthy of respect.
If anything is excellent or worthy of praise, think about
those kinds of things."
Philippians 4:11

Stephanie Uelese Jackson is a single parent of 2 teenage boys. She currently lives in the beautiful Aloha State of Hawaii. Ua Mau ke Ea Oka 'Aina I ka Pono Hawaiian for "The life of the land is perpetuated in righteousness." She has made Hawaii her home raising both her children. They have come to embrace the culture and diversity Hawaii.

Stephanie is a guest service agent for the hotel industry, contributing to the Aloha spirit in our tourist industry. She enjoys meeting people that have traveled near and far to enjoy the warm weather and beautiful beaches. Her latest accomplishment is her poem entry for Spiritual Writer Network. As a first time writer Stephanie is so blessed to hear that her poem has been selected to be published in the Spiritual Writers Poetry Contest Book. Praise God for the opportunity for her to write and express herself. She attends the poetry readings at Hawaii Slams located at Fresh Café Kaka'ako every first Thursday of the month. She enjoys hearing poetry from people of all ages, culture, experience, maturity and simplicity. She is a staff member of the Assembly of God Hawaii Samoan Section Newsletter "Ole Alaga." She is currently writing the sports section for the newsletter and is working on an article called School is in Session for their upcoming Newsletter scheduled to be published in September.

When she's not working or writing she enjoys the company of her family and playing tourist around the island. Pretending to be first time visitors to the island and blending with the tourist is exciting and entertaining. There's never a dull moment when you're on vacation! Stephanie hopes to continue to write and be a blessing to others thru her writings and if it's God's will through public speaking. Stephanie thanks everyone for their words of encouragement, support and love. You may reach her at <u>*sujackson808@gmail.com.*</u>

Enchanted Place

by Brandi Hale

Take me to an enchanted place,
Where the caterpillars lay and the gazelles play.
Where the sun shines boldly off the waters rushing the
bay,
Like the flowers bloom in the month of May.

Take me to an enchanted place,
Where all mankind can come together and stay,
As we magnify Him every day,
Remembering the blood He shed that sacred day,
Lord have mercy upon me as I pray.

Show me the way today,
To touch lives in every way.
Give me a word to say,
To show love all through the day.
Surrounded by your grace I shall stay,
Peace I will continually portray.
That one day I may enter this enchanted place,
In your name I pray.
Amen.

Brandi Hale is a native of Arizona and has written as a volunteer writer for Teen Graffiti Magazine and a freelance writer for various agencies.

Sanctuary

by Kev Milsom

He built fantasy locations using mental imagery,
making many sites for solitude, planned indefinitely.
For years content to be alone, sat deep within his dreams,
through times when life was constant cruel –
to mask insecure screams.
Staying here ever-frequently, lonely but content;
living in a child's playground, never paying adult rent.
Dining frequently on mango bread and peanut butter
cake,
relaxed amongst technicolour grass, swum deep in vodka
lakes.
Yet deep…
   deep down inside…
      a lonely soul's cries were heard.

She burst into his world, like a comet from the sky;
a bright, creative source of light; an awesome, natural
high.
Him, so long a castaway, moored upon secluded beach,
while solitude grew peaceful roots -
it taught him not to reach.
But when she landed in his world and walked along the
sand,
his mind in mighty awe as he let her hold his hand.
Suddenly no place for fearful things he used to see and
hear,
just room for friendship truly deep; companionship so
dear.
So deep…
   deep down inside…
      two lonely soul's cries were heard.

Their humour shining brightly strong, smiles illuminating
all round
in radiant pools of warmth, to light up Earth's darkest
ground.
Sat at night to watch faint stars of distant fire,
Both joined together in new-formed land –
built by twinned hearts' desires.
The world holds much more purpose now, walking side by
side,
to compensate for when they'd begged the universe and
cried.
Now each dwells within a larger heart – today and
evermore;
blessed was the day she made him whole and landed on his
shore.
For deep…
    deep down inside…
        our cries are always heard.

Kev Milsom is in his very early 50's and divides his time between studying and writing. He is currently in the first of four years of study within Metaphysics and hopes to train as a hypnotherapist next year – his overriding goal being to further develop areas of spiritual healing and build some form of career around helping people. He plans to do this alongside some dear friends who also share the same goals. In this, he is ever-hopeful of a lottery win to help him achieve personal ambitions, although – judging from his karmic lessons – he believes this to be highly unlikely.

All Is All

by Linda Kay Murphy

The only life I know includes shadow.
It is only in darkness
That I can truly be still enough to see.

It is only alone in darkness
That new awakenings are born.

Give me not the platitudes of happy folk.
Give me these things only:
>   Breath enough to fill my lungs,
>   Light enough to continue walking,
>   Butterflies enough to remember transformation,
>   Courage enough to let Creation find me.

Do not proclaim me ungodly for refusing false hope,
Do not proclaim me insane for embracing mystery.

The Great "I Am"
Is exactly where I am.
All expression is saintly.
All life is holy.

*Linda Kay Murphy has a B.A. in Human Development, is a
graduate of the National Holistic Institute of Therapeutic Massage
& Health Education, and is an ordained minister. Her poetry has
been published in "Shadow Poetry's Best of 2003", "Tower of
Faith" Long Island Publishing, and she won an Honorable Mention
from Writer's Digest for her first book of original poems called "All
the Vulnerable Joys" (available on Amazon). Poetry has always
been her first choice for creative expression of spirit and authentic self.*

This Light

by Kathleen "Kat" Regan

As of late,
Sacred Invitations
have been casting
an abundance of Light
upon my shadows.

Shadows that follow me wherever I go.
Shadows that, somehow, still manage to
blind me to the Light.

Light persistent in its pursuit
for sure
yet
it is still Light
that must struggle
with my shadows.

Shadows forged in fear,
steeled in rage.
Decades spent in armored,
self-groomed defense
against having any hope.

You see,
once upon a time,
the tunnel I lived in
seemed to offer
no light
at its end
and hope's path
can't be seen
in such absolute

darkness.

So, ironic this Light then
that still, valiantly, pierces and
fends off my shadows,
resolute in breaking through
via some new cracks
in my heart.
Light that catches
in my throat and
turns and twists
in my gut.

Light that calls out to me
"BREATHE!"
when I find myself
struggling to take
the next breath.

This Light,
standing strong
against my shadows,
again and again and again,
reminding me I would have
no shadows
without it.

When all else fails
I must remember
This Light
does not,
will not,
perhaps cannot,
abandon ...

This Light that, somehow,
fought its way in ...

into my tunnel.
This Light that was, finally,
not an illusion at
my tunnel's end ...

This Light that reminds resolutely
It is not an illusion ...

The tunnel is.

Kathleen (aka Kat) is a Sixth Sensory Intuitive, Certified Usui and Karuna Reiki Master/Teacher and a Certified Level IV Transformational Breath Worker through The School of Integrative Psychology, as well as a graduate of the school's intensive 3-Year Master of Integrative Psychology program.

As a Group Leader, Lecturer, award-winning Poet and Author of the book "Promises Kept: A Journey Out of the Darkness Into the Light," her approach focuses on integrating body, breath, and energy work to reclaim and honor the body/mind/spirit connection.

For over 21 years, Kat's use of her ongoing holistic training and expertise also incorporates, when appropriate, aromatherapy, writing, movement, song, and/or imagery as tools to connect to the Divine within us all. Her ministry also includes creating and officiating personalized wedding ceremonies with the intention of creating a unique experience for each couple she marries.

Autumn Prayer

by Patricia Randall Berry

Oh God
your vibrant blanket covers me
walking under your canopy of colors
the fog kisses my skin
as it lifts off the water in the morning sun,
exposing your grand reflection in the rippling wind

You shine, dance, peek through the pines, maples, and
elms
On the rutted trail of broken roots, jagged rocks, and dark
shadows,
my feet stop
my eyes close
and I hear your glory.

You call me
like music of a trickling brook
until the falls pound
the rhythmic sounds of autumn
"Come, come my child, follow me"

Patricia Randall Berry is a poet and educator who finds her inspiration in the history and day-to-day experience of her family, community, and the presence of God in the natural world. As a graduate of Colby-Sawyer College with a degree in psychology, she is the Christian Education Director at Mattapoisett Congregational Church in Mattapoisett, where she is building an environment that encourages spiritual curiosity while exploring the traditions and commitments of an active faith. While studying for Commissioned Ministry in the United Church of Christ, she is also writing poetry, vignettes, and historical fiction for young readers. She lives with her husband and three children in southeastern Massachusetts.

My Wish for You

by Debbie Quigley

That you find that person who hugs you on good days and bad ones!
A person that loves who you are!
Is the shoulder you cry on and lean on
A person that never hurts your feelings
Makes you never feel lonely
Shares your laughter
Shares your dreams
Is proud of you each and every day
With whatever accomplishments you make
Or strive for!
Holds your hand on the dark days and on the light ones!
One that promises hold true!
My wish for you!
They are always that warm hug
One that holds you and your heart
My wish for you!

Debra Quigley born in Peterborough Ontario Canada Mother of two sons. Debra published Wind Whispers a Poetry Anthology a collection of poetry based on life lessons. She also contributed in Touched By an Angel, The Best of 2013 also Whispers of The Soul along with many talented writers chosen in Spiritual Writers Network contest publications. Debra currently resides in a small country hamlet she enjoys nature and gardening. Debra's poetry is simple and real she loves to touch hearts with her words. One reader One heart One word is her quote when writing poetry. If you wish to purchase Wind Whispers it is available in 3-book and print version at http://www.amazon.com/author/debbiequigley

Maggie's Song of Prayer

Midnight Reflections of a Caregiver's Heart

by Margaret Honnold

Journal entry for November 7, 2012

Help me Lord, to know the way, this has been a grueling day, night approaches and with it comes the tears. I hate it when the sun goes down, and evening shadows come around, and the shadows of my heart overflow my mind.

But as you hear my sighs you know, when people's lives are shredded so, without peace in mind or heart. So hold me Lord, and I will stay, touched by you in every way, clinging to your steadfast, perfect plan.

I don't know what I would do, were it not for the thought of you, hearing what my voice can't bear to say. So, once again as night comes in, I will take your hand and then, know that in this house your presence dwells.

During day they're pushed away, I am able to survive and stay, but once alone the voices fill my mind. The critics who come loudest are the ones I've loved the most. They have chosen to abandon me and sometimes even boast.

They say in seeking help for me, I'm selfish and don't care, about the man, who disappears and is generally unaware. The clanging the of their criticism causes my legs to shake, my foundation of dependence on those I've loved just breaks.

"You can't do this, oh, don't do that, I don't agree, I hate you" - my best is never good enough and in judgment, they forsake me.

But hold me Lord, and I will stay, touched by you in every way clinging to your steadfast and perfect plan. I don't know what I would do, were it not for the thought of you, hearing what my voice can't bear to say. So, once again as night comes in, I will take your hand and then, know that in this house your presence dwells.

What is right for the one I love? I can't do it all, but I know Lord, into your arms my unsteady life can fall. For it is when I fight the tears, hold my breath and face my fears, I seek you knowing that you're here. My fear abates, my aching wanes, and time begins to move again and I know tomorrow holds a brand new day.

Let your loving arms surround my heart, your whispered words uphold me, and I will cling tight to you this night, and calmly wait and see. For in my head I've always known you hold the perfect plan, and though my future stands far off, my heart will understand.

I'll not worry what daytime brings just get me through tonight and step-be-step I'll move ahead and try to do what's right. So, once again as night comes in, I will take your hand and then, know that in this house your presence dwells.

So, once again as night comes in, I will take your hand and then, know that in this house your presence dwells.

So, once again as night comes in, I will take your hand and then, know that in this house your presence dwells...

"I Margaret dwell in the shelter of the Most High God and I say of the Lord, He is my strength...my ever present help in time of trouble... for surely he will save me from fowler's snare, and from the deadly pestilence. He will uphold me with his strong right hand, that my foot might not strike the stone and that I might live out all my life as ordained in Psalm 91." Amen

Margaret Honnold is a registered nurse living in a small mid-western town with her 4 rescued Basset Hounds. She is active in community and church volunteer activities and enjoys "tooting her own horn" in a local community band. She has written regular columns for 2 church newsletters, writes prophetically as the Lord leads and shares her journal entries on Facebook with her many friends. She is currently completing a memoir about caring for her husband who died of complications from Alzheimer's Dementia.

Paint Me a Picture, God!

by Susie Tierney

Paint me a picture, God!
    Let Your palette of colors splash across my
landscape!

Paint me a picture of summer!
    Use green – lots of green;
        grass-green, caterpillar-green, thunderstorm-
green.
    Use red – lots of red;
        sunset-red, cardinal-red, clay-red.
    Use yellow, too – lots of yellow;
        duckling-yellow, daffodil-yellow, sunshine-
yellow.

Paint me a picture of autumn, God!
    Use brown – lots of brown;
        open-field brown, tree-trunk brown, dead-leaf
brown.
    Use orange, too – lots of orange;
        harvest-moon orange, corn-stock orange,
pumpkin pie orange.

Paint me a picture of winter, God!
    Use grey – lots of grey;
        wolf-grey, overcast-grey, bare-branch grey.
    Use blue, too – lots of blue;
        cloud-blue, ice-water blue, winter-scarf blue.

Paint me a picture of spring, God!
    Use pink – lots of pink;
        rose-petal pink, newborn-pink, thunderstorm-
pink.

Use gold, too – lots of gold;
    mari-gold, butterfly-gold, sunrise-gold.

Paint me a picture, God!
    Let Your palette of colors splash across my
landscape!

Susie Tierney is the Executive Director of the Center for Social Ministry in Des Moines, Iowa. Susie coordinates poverty awareness and justice education programs; is a member of the Des Moines Area Religious Council Board of Directors; and is an Associate of the Sisters of St. Francis in Dubuque, Iowa.

The Body's Reply

by Alethea Kehas

You see, Child of the Mind
I cannot lie

When you let go of constriction
I follow the moon-tide

Old blood releases
to return Her light

Whoever said the moon is man
lies to hold fear in thrall

Enchantment is a misunderstood
power of denial

The magic to being
is coded in every cell I hold

When you divide anger with forgiveness
you receive abundance

I play by simple math

The product of tolerance
minus hate is love

These rules you have created
only impede our growth

Would you starve a child if you knew
she lived inside the hunger of your heart?

Give her the breath you trap
it is enough to feed her

To understand infinity free the wings
you have tied behind my back

Reunion is simple addition
after you learn the rules of subtraction

*Alethea Kehas is a poet, writer and owner of Inner Truth Healing.
She lives in Bow, NH with her family of 4 humans plus 4 animals,
which yields the promise of infinity and balance in 8.*

Words from Gran

by Ellen Palmer

'I never wanted to get old,' said Gran
'I disliked the other choice,
on balance I'll take these damn aches and pains.'
she laughed in her faded voice.

Her hair still thick with unpermed curls,
framed her wrinkles etched by pain,
'I've lost so many I have loved
but in dreams they come back again.'

I wish I'd known way back then
how much I'd miss them so.
I wish I'd taken time to savour
each and every little rainbow.

'I'll never fly to Acapulco,
I've had to set my limits,
but I've learnt to value every day
and every moment in it.'

'I don't expect you'll listen,'
She shared with eyes, clear and blue.
'But before you get as old as me,
I hope you know it's true.'

The Rebirth of Love...

by Lydia Fraser

Lying in the womb of the shadow-realms
Immersed in an embryonic substance
A paradoxical climate of nurturing and entrapment
The incubation phase of a paradigm shift

Ignorant to my growth, deceptively dormant,
entwined within the life force of my being
The ego retracted due to my fragility
An implosion of the self occurred...

The synergistic point of soul retrieval
My underworld seduction ceased
The cauldron, barren of primordial water,
as the creative flame continued to burn...

Baptismal fire, reawakened desire
Lying in the ashes of my former self
My ancient spirit emerged in a pristine state
Unchanged, yet transformed...

Everything is an experience to love ourselves more
Transform from carbon ashes, to our crystalline core
Universal rebirth is our divine gift
We are all in the process of making this shift

From the pain of duality, to the unity of love
We wipe the dust of hell-fire from our wings
The heavens are opening, as we open to our innocence...
Into the celestial embrace of one heart

Absolution

by Jessica Wierman

A soul, wandering alone, yet seeking
A companion as fantastic as what has been found
Locking the day's door to remain forever bound.
A fantasy that exists
Tangible, within grasp
Like drops of dew falling through outstretched hands.
A panicking plummet, or an undetermined land
Preparation inconceivable under nameless command.
Trepidation manifesting monsters, savagery
An overwhelming reality
Desperately seeking the memory
Of dreams turned earthly.
A battle within, lost in the wind
Or adrift on the sea
Like so many others that were not yet meant to be.
Damage of war viewed through misguided eyes
Ignorant to the absolution of time.
Vehement patience,
The sole pedagogue
A testament to the purpose of life;
Continuing motion, full of energy
Each moment an opportunity
To change everything.

Remembering Love

by Wyshika Gibson

Love opens hearts in so many ways
Its truth reveals the authentic from the fake
Shows up at the most inopportune times
Never hidden yet at times it may be hard to find
Usually found in the most unexpected places
Unannounced, its presence stands out
Love surpasses and endures through heart break and pain
It teaches, it listens and it creates
Unable to be measured or defined
Better experienced than explained
Communicates without a single word
It renews, it's vibrant and bold
Love is unconditional and free
It falls into place, it will just be
It's not insecure, non-judgmental or manipulative
Brings balance with a natural flow, radiates an amazing
glow
With Love, there's no comparison because of its true and
deep connection
It's universal and transparent
It sees beyond color and race
Love is not destructive nor does it envy
It's kind and caring
Has its own beauty
It's constant and calm
Takes its time because patience is its key
Love is sincere, it never pretends

It encourages you to be your true self
 Love can be represented and expressed in varies ways
Expressed through art, music, nature, a simple touch, or a kind heart
Represented by our families, great moments, and shared memories
Love heals and helps you to let go and forgive
It gives hope and brings compassion
It's a beaming light in dark places
Inspires risks and positive change
Reasons for sleepless nights, late night awakenings, and deep thinking
Love brings joy and peace
Produces smiles and laughs
Love opens up your world to new possibilities
Starts new chapters and new beginnings in your life
And even if love is lost or gained
In a special place is where love will always remain
Remembering Love

Wyshika Gibson is a proud mother, poet, and author. She discovered her passion for writing at an earlier age. She has tapped back into her gift of writing in hopes that her writing will inspire and help people heal and grow. She enjoys writing non-fiction and poetry. She self-published her first book in February 2014. Some of her poems have been featured in SWN's "Touch by An Angel", "The Best of Spiritual Writers 2013", "Whispers of the Soul: A Poetry Anthology", "The Best of Spiritual Writers 2014", and The New Age News Magazine November 2013/April 2014 Edition. She loves reading, writing, and spending time with her family. She is currently working on other writing projects.

Contact: wyshikagibson@gmail.com

Love

by Paula A. Lesiak

What is Love?
It is a creation that never fails
Led by the spirit, I'll go into deeper details
It pierces the soul and goes deeper than anything
A melody it makes in the heart, a beautiful song it sings
People search for that feeling to make them feel whole
Nothings' greater than love, by my God it is told
It covers wounds, heartaches and pain
When God embraces you that's the greatest gain
We are let down by someone we love day after day
The love of God picks us up and takes the burden away
We dance when happy and sadness brings a flood of tears
Jesus loves us, He's faithful, he'll remove our fears
We have to love one another as he has commanded us to
do
We can't go wrong by being obedient to a God that's true
He carried the cross and died for us from the beginning
He is the true meaning of love, now, forever and even in
the ending

I thank my Lord & Savior Jesus for being my inspiration. I have three sons, Terry Jarez & Byron. I also thank The Ministry Of Power In Evangelism, my church family, for always encouraging me to do what God has chosen me to do. I dedicate this poem to Donnie Batts, the special man in my life & the Howell Family in Jesus Name.

Love's Return

by Jo Mills

Ancient eyes watch light's descent
as snow falls, or petals of lilies
imprint the Age's shift

We remember
fields bathed in star-sheen
riverways of violet glow
skies a bowl of dawning gold
rose-scent seas awash

We remember
calls melding tones of bliss
as shadow-plays dissolve
from imaginary walls
sounds of carefree laughter

We remember
light-flakes brushing our faces
sinking through skin and cell
heart touching heart
across time's old traces
weaving lines of light

We are love's long-waited return

Jo Mills is a poet, writer, and 'anchor' during Gaia's Shift into higher frequencies of light and love. She lives in the beautiful Perth hills with her teenage son, two cheeky rabbits and a flock of birds. Jo writes fantasy/science fiction novels and short stories as Joanna Fay, and has an author site at http://joannafay.me/
Jo is also an ET 'contactee' and shares her experiences, communications and spiritual practices at http://heartstar.org/

The Hardest Path

by Jeanelle Morneau

Walking down a path,
On a warm spring day.
Filled with determination,
Because you knew there was no other way.

So many voices as you walk,
Many are cheering, while others cry,
Carrying that heavy load,
You know, it's nearly time... to die.

A deadly crown adorns your head,
Feeling thorns push through, you almost dread,
But despite the pain, you carry on with love,
Knowing who watches from above.

Scarlet lines cover your back,
As the world threatens to fade to black,
The path slopes up and you ascend,
To the place that will soon mark your end.

Your wooden load is taken then,
But you still bear the weight of sin,
You never sinned, you're white as snow,
But the righteous path is very thin.
You are the way the world can take,
To a place where the devil won't ever win.

Soldiers surround you on the hill,
As a sharpened spike is placed,
The hammer strikes and in it goes,
With more pain than you've ever faced.

The cross is raised up to the Sun,
and in agony you wait,
The battle for life is almost won,
As you fulfill your fate.

With one last cry,
You close your eyes, and die.
Your body is placed in a tomb,
And a stone is rolled in place.
In darkness you lie still,
Of life there is no trace.

Three days pass in silence,
With nobody aware,
Your death was not your end at all!
The plan was made with care.

You rise to life in glory,
The only trace of death your scars,
This begins another story,
One that has no need for worry.
You are alive, and always will be,
For your kingdom you offer the key.

You took the hardest path there was,
And your only reason was because,
You love every person in creation,
And want to add them to your nation.

My name is Jeanelle Morneau. I am 16 years old and I was 15 when I wrote this poem. I love to write poetry, especially concerning different Bible events. My goal for this poem is to show people what Christ went through from a unique point of view, so people will remember that the crucifixion is not just another story, and his sacrifice should never be taken for granted.

My Amazing Man

by Cheryl Denise Chandler

Nanny, Nanny, Nan, Nan.
I accepted Jesus Hand.
Infinity styled costumed made ring.
My heart is filled with so much joy.
Forever I will have a lovely song to sing.

My Wedding Dress.
An Original Designers Special.
Made with a Beautiful Spirit.
My veil is made of the finest of Faith.
My shoes were designed by Grace.
My train I received as a gift.
It was given to me by Mercy.

A Living Prince.
Also He's the King.
What more can a woman ask for?.
I am so glad I decided to answer my front door.
Just to think I almost didn't.
Thinking it was the paperboy.

The song that will be played at our reception will be
Hosanna.
My Amazing Man really asked for my hand.

Jesus hands down you are my very best.
Oh how I adore you.
Jesus I really love you.
"Yes Father God."
"I DO"

Writing is a gift that only a loving God can bring.
This most important endowment is spiritually soothing.
Being at one in that anointed space of creativity.
A thirst quenching realm I pray to forever lounge in.
Spiritually connected I always want to be with the gift of writing.
In Jesus precious name........
Amen.

My name is Cheryl Denise Chandler, I have been writing for as long as I can remember. My very first publishing was in 1979 through the YWCA. The gift of writing for me is spiritually soothing.

Using various personal life experiences as my canvas. It's my passion to infuse life encouraging poetry. Writings, they'll breathe into every single reader, the very essence of hope, love, inspiration and understanding.

Meditation on a Tree After Storm

by Ethan Phibbs

It's not the storm I'm interested in;
not the tumult of wild things below electric spasms,
not the sullen winds angling torrents of nutrient essentials
into sympathetic lands like passionate blessings.

It's the other side of frenzy I want,
the supreme repose of after-storm.

Dark green crowns drooping in sheens
of lucent bulbs, manifold leaves fervent
and stationary, meditating drunk in gratification.

Sometimes I'll imagine myself as the tree with no season
by which to shed myself, or grow impeded
by an overturned blue bowl.

My existence would be pale roots extending
the length of a single grain, each stemmed page
a poem singing the spirits Source.

It's the otherside of after-storm I seek,
passionate blessings above electric spasms.

Connectedness

by Seraphina Phileo-Noor

I do not seek Fame, Wealth or Recognition.
What I seek is the Divine Love of the Father...
I feel most content when I am connected and
In Tune with my Soul.
When I FEEL the presence of God in my Being.
When I cannot stop crying because I know that I am being
guided in my life...
The PURITY of my being is elevated to a state of
substantial Mercy and in that moment I no longer care
about my life or what this world has to offer.
I feel that the greater calling is to live a life that progresses
to the Light and ultimately arrives at its intended
destination.
I want to live a PURPOSE FILLED LIFE...
The contentment I feel when I am in that state of
"ONENESS" is indescribable ...Why????
Because it's unique, it's intense.
It's unifying the Mind, Body and Spirit to a state of
awareness and awesomeness.
The stillness and silence in Meditation that promulgates
my Soul to open up to heal my Mind and Body as well as
my life, can only be achieved when I relegate my mortal
self to God.
In that moment I feel an overwhelming sense of Peace
that can only be described as pure Bliss...
For I know who my redeemer is.
I know who the key to my happiness is.
I know who will continue to guide me and inspire me
every day.
I know that I will continue on my journey and will expand
my knowingness of the LIGHT as I understand it.
But I cannot do it alone because I will be guided every step

of the way.
I do not seek Fame, Wealth or Recognition.
What I seek is the ultimate reward.
The Divine Love of the Father, which has already led me
to the opening and connection of my SOUL......

I was born and brought up in a fundamentalist Christian family in Humacao, Puerto Rico. We are a family of five: my parents, me, my sister and my younger brother. My earliest childhood recollections was one full of wonderment and curiosity. I remember between the ages of 5 through 12 years old asking myself certain questions. Wanting to know why was I here on this earth? What was my purpose or reason for living? These and many other questions would dominate my mind all the way up to my adulthood. As I look back at my life now I completely understand the importance of my longing and yearning. These questions were my initiation to my spiritual exploration and thus my journey began. A journey that has brought me from being raised Christian with a mother who is a Pentecostal Minister. To a Mystic Medium, Channeler and just a vessel of God. I now understand the meaning of embracing the Gifts that have been bestowed upon me. This journey has awaken the deepest desires of my soul. It has awaken the Light that was missing in my life. My spiritual journey has opened me up to the divine presence within myself, the God in me, the Light in me and the Presence of the most high God!!! This is my truth and this is my reality....

Amtrak Rides and Spring Disguised

by Sara Sass

The stretch of blooms
For the touch of bees-
Even if the rohypnol clouds
Killed them all. Honey's dead.

And yet the white purple petals
Reach to soak up sun.
Not knowing they're the last.
Not knowing they're the only one.

A flower wasting in dark dirt
With nothing left to quench it,
Except the sun slow burning out
And the ocean: rising, rising.

All your hidden keyhole wonders
Build bridges,
Write symphonies,
Inspire men and mountains.

But can't utter no
In a crowded tram car
Suspended in sweet darkness--

Bitter turned to blood.

Piano jaws came unhinged
In his eyes.
Southern water lapped at his mouth.
Clear grain alcohol smothered all doubt.

Rocketing north on a silver train
With the stones of industry cast aside,
He spoke of Japanese women
Never answering where he had been.

Love for Writing

by Swati Mittal

On one lonely evening,

As my emotions went haywire,

I grabbed a paper and pen,

In hope to clear my mind.

And that particular evening,

I discovered my love for writing.

Writing is a road trip,

An exploration of unknown lands.

Writing is as peaceful as a,

Midnights stroll on a moon-lit beach.

It's an extension of a writer's soul,

The very blood flowing in his veins.

It's as exciting as the first kiss,

As captivating as the first love.

A feeling of adrenaline rush,

Like having done the Everest Summit.

Writing is a gateway to another world,

A license to unrestricted dreaming,

Like a horse without a harness,

Galloping around the green fields.

Writing was my first love,

It's My dream, My passion, My hope.

Writing is who I am,

Without it I would be a lost soul...

Hi my name is Swati Mittal I love to write poetry and have been doing it ever since I was a kid. Poetry is like the blood running in my veins. I wish to build a career in the writing field as a novelist and poet. Being selected into this contest for publication is a big thing for me, this is my first step to success. I am very thankful to Spiritual Writers Network and Transcendent Publishing for having shortlisted my poem and giving me this wonderful chance of having my work published for the first time.

If you enjoyed reading my works and would like to read more you can find my other works at my blog ' https://athoughtdifferent.wordpress.com/ ' or you can also contact me personally at swatimittal1994@gmail.com

December Nights

by Jared Rhodes

The feel of the glass by its touch should tip you off of
what's in store today.

                  Cold weather, my favorite type.

The joy of the change is not what warms me in this season
of freeze.

                        What's

coming is better.

A time to be with brother, father, sister, mother enjoying
the break that's received.

                The tenth day of the twelfth

month.

As we grow the gifts are less important than giving to
someone who has none

                because we know how blessed we

are.

What's more about this heavy coat forecast is the time to
reflect on the year that has past

                        for we are

nearing the end.

This trip around the sun has given us many things to
celebrate and recall

            but also things to forget.

Maybe that's why such a time of cheer is so close to the
last 24 hours

              when we finally change out that

calendar.

I was always told to spend my nights wisely, so at home I
will be until that 365th day comes

                    and this

year is behind me.

The Rainbow Promise

by Janet R. Sady

Sodden clouds hide sunrays.
Fear reigns as days drift past.
Spirits droop and salty rain falls
from grief-stricken eyes.
Where's the warmth
of golden light?
The peace which only
the Son can bring?
Look up! He's there—
Waiting for us to trust
in Him again and claim
the rainbow promise.

**"I do set my bow in the cloud and
It shall be for a token of a covenant
between me and the earth." Genesis 9:13**

Janet R. Sady - author, poet, story teller and motivational speaker. Certified lay speaker in the United Methodist Church. Published in anthologies-- Including: Reflections of the Soul, Love &Light, Falling in Love with You, I Choose You, The Best of Spiritual Writers' Network, Secret Place, Penned from the Heart, Patchwork Path (2 issues). Magazines: Country Woman, True Story, Our USA Magazine, Country Woman, Alamance and Loyalhanna Review Magazines as well as newspapers and other magazines. Received best of show for fiction, and blue ribbon for non-fiction in the Silver Arts Competition in 2013. She has won awards for poetry and short stories. Author of six books- God's Lessons from Nature, God's Parables and Lessons Book 2, Sacagewea-The Bird Woman, Mr. Bernie's Most Favorite Place, The Great American Dream,

and   Winston   Wants   a   Home   for   Christmas.
janfran@windstream.net or jansady422.wordpress.com

The Yogi

by Jake Teeny

Only children know
that he wasn't just smarter
than the average bear,
a clever cibophile
in search of pic-a-nic
baskets; but a practitioner
of ancient
beliefs, an ardent ascetic
who earned his title
helping those forest wanderers
discard their bamboo
sheathed burdens.
—*Ommm*—
He sought *moksha*,
his wearied legs crossed,
callused paws asleep on his knees,
where beneath the shade
of a redwood he meditated
on how one could have a collar
without a shirt.

Jake Teeny received M.A. in social psychology, and is currently pursuing a PhD in the field at Ohio State University. When not conducting research, he tirelessly works on his fiction, plays basketball competitively (at least in his head), and lists things in groups of three. Links to his published work and awards as well as his weekly blog, "Psychophilosophy Tips for Everyday Living," can be found at his website, www.JakeTeeny.com

You Are What the Angels Praise

by Maureen Addington

You are what the angels praise. You are that.
One with all that is. There is nothing You are not.
You abide in the destination that is never left.

Whatever arises You are that,
And You are the player of that,
And You have lived through the appearance of that,
Without ever having taken a single step.

All action arises out of You.
You are held by the sublime Love that You are created
from.
Every cell and vibrant particle is suffused with God that is
You.

You are brave beyond measure.
You traverse the illusion of separation.
All manifestation resides already played out inside Your
own Heart.

This One, the Reunion that was never separate,
Is the strength of Isness,
The pure Love of how things are in their ever-present
Perfection.

All this has arisen and subsided in the eternity that You are
without end.
You are what is always here,
Without condition,
In complete freedom to be or do whatever arises,
Flawlessly,
With pure support,

The Heart of all Creation, The Beloved, The immortal One.

What God intimates, breathes, speaks and acts has always and forever been You.

I'm challenging the paradigm. Just between us bios are funny. They're written in 3rd person by the person themselves and filled with awards and recognition. What's the point of all that but to rob you, the reader, of your own discernment. Read my poems or not, be drawn to them or not. Use your own heart to decide. Don't let what's happened before, or someone else's opinions influence you. Let your own inner God have its experience. I certainly did when I wrote them.

Ode to the Nature in your Nascence

by Jaime Paterson

Shake your hair- you are the ever-weeping willow.
And while sometimes you feel starless,
Galaxies do dance in your irises.
You have hills on your forehead and valleys in your thighs.
I promise I have never seen anything as meaningful.

You walk softer and louder than God,
These cracked heels like drinking deserts,
These bony ankles like the widest trunk.
Split wrists, I promise you this:
The Mississippi spells less secrets than these.

Whitened knees like tectonic plates-
You are the force that glaciers cower beneath.
Your thunder hips crack and roll-
They are what demons pray to and
Angels long for.

Like restitution, your tears are petrichor,
And you seethe like wildfire in your anger.
Parted lips, parched like sea-drift,
Your thick smile feels like red wine and
Welcoming cities, arms wide like rip tide.

Your roiling body resembles early earth,
And when you feel poiseless, I promise,
Nothing in you is poisonous.
Corrode your own erosion, darling,
Let there be no sound.

Indecision

by Silvana Redden

Two equal strengths stand at war in my mind;

Each doles mental torture more cruel and unkind.

The noisy clock —dreadful villain! – shouts out each tick

To make me more aware of what must be made —QUICK!

I've a notion to run. I don't think I can take it,

But it *is* my decision and, alone, I must make it.

My head throbs in agony of irresolution.

My heart thumps in my effort to find the solution.

The quest sears my senses, while the blatant clock

Trumpets oncoming gloom with its blaring tick-tock

But my burning brain blanks with each minute's pass

While dark falls like sand in my mind's hour glass.

Then, lo: midst the turmoil, I encounter light!

Oh, Heartquake: be still, and oh. Tension: take flight!

No more does the clock tick so painfully fast,

For I've reached my verdict, and I'm free at last!

But —deep in my thoughts – there still lurks in the shade

Grave doubts for the morrow 'bout decisions I've made.

In Amante Novum (The New Lover)

by Christine Sue Cheng

He has a beautiful, tortured soul,

He has many lovers, but the world must never know,

Our hidden passions - a fantasy,

At night, we let them transform into reality.

He tells tall tales with vigour,

His kisses, his touch - they trigger

A release of undiscovered, intense feeling,

Love or lust - he has me reeling.

Christine Sue Cheng Chan currently lives and works in Novi Sad, Serbia. She was born and educated in the UK and moved to Australia as a teenager, where she studied Diplomas in Business Administration and Information Technology. She was married in 2005 in Melbourne and has one daughter. She always had a keen interest in English Language and English Literature but her career was established in the areas of IT and Administration.

She migrated to Serbia with her family in 2011. Since her divorce in 2014 she started to write poetry as a new hobby and 'In Amante Novum' is the first of her poems to be published.

Dreaming Son

by Emily Day

Though all babies are welcomed
As cherubs and innocent things
All are born of circumstance
Starving soldiers or spoiled kings.
Some children sip from silver spoons
And others taste spoons of lead.
Some mothers pinch round, chubby cheeks
Others cannot keep them fed.
I know my child's only fault
Is that he was born to me.
Destined never to witness Rome,
Due to my own poverty.
I tell my son what mothers do,
That he can do all he dreams,
But late at night, I bury tears
For someone told that to me.
I look into his eyes like mine,
And wish I'd set my lover free
So he had found a finer half
And loved someone more than me.
I too was born from circumstance,
I too was careful to dream
But still I dream for my son,
Most of all, that he is more than me.

I am a 22 year old student. I have lived near Detroit for all my life, and I've been writing poetry for six years, never published. I enjoy writing about the perspective of the lower-middle class, as I feel it's a unique experience not well represented in poetry. My dream is to travel the world after I graduate.

Sunday Dinner

by Naomi Tene' Austin

I am hungry for **You;**
Seeking nourishment in formal institutions,
programs,
bulletins,
and orders of service.

I enter your gates with thanksgiving,
greeted happily by warm embraces and familiar faces.
This is my safe haven.
Here, I am validated.

I commemorate this weekly gala donning nothing less than
Sunday's best.
Impeccably tailored,
coiffed,
branded,
and accessorized,
Affirming nods let me know I have met their approval.

I clap my hands on cue and faithfully pay my due to
remain in good standing.
This ritual tastes comforting like…
Sunday Dinner.
But where is the guest of honor?

Napkin placed on lap, I await your arrival;
While secretly coveting my neighbor's fullness.
They are content with the experience as I am starved for
your presence.
I am dissatisfied with this plentiful buffet of religious
cliché,
Still,

This I Do in Remembrance of **You**.

It's hard to sleep on an empty stomach.
Faithfully **You** awaken me at the crack of dawn for my
morning sustenance.
I lay here allowing **You** to utter grace in my ear as you
prepare my spread.
I thank **You** aloud while eagerly dressing for our regularly
scheduled activity
I step outside and we meet again as you utter discernment
upon the wind.

I feel **You** in my legs as they alternate right, left, right, left
propelling me forward in exploration of these city streets.
I see **You** in the innocence of the infant sitting
comfortably in stroller as mommy awaits the Metro.

I recognize **You** in the vacant gaze of the homeless fellow
nearby
And I beam with joy as we exchange glances, mutually
acknowledging your presence in one another.

I slow my jog to a halt and observe **You** in the lake.
That's **You** there moving in the direction of the water's
flow.
You, in the morning dew that kisses my skin.

I drink **You** into my pores.
You wash over me in the breeze and I'm baptized in your
love.
I offer a tear of gratitude as Your presence envelopes me.

Africa

by Sue J Daniels

AFRICA

Hear me!

If I could speak to you I would say;

You watch me swaddled in sweating, tattered rags as mucus dries on my face, up my nose, feeding a thousand flies that swarm in an around my big beautiful brown eyes.

They are the only part of my soul not yet dead, but slowly dying, I just need water, my mother needs water so that she might make milk to nourish me.

Water, a small amount of water might just allow me to survive yet another minute or even a whole day in this filthy stinking place, where death here is as common as a cold there.

I don't mind the flies; they have become part of me, and the part of me that reminds me I'm alive.

You watch on your big screens and you give, just a bit, you give and I live.

I dream that I will be able to play in the shade in the dirt in a bright yellow frilly dress sent by you.

NORTH OF ENGLAND

My sweet child, If I could get to you now I would make you a cup of my finest Yorkshire Tea in one of the bone china cup and saucers that Bill and I were given as part of a wedding present 52 years ago.

Fifty two years of ups and downs, having beautiful babies just like you - not starving like you - thirsty like you but beautiful like you.
Now at eighty-two, a widow of ten years I watch the birds feeding from the myriad of feeders placed carefully around the garden.

A bit of television at lunchtime - in my now pointless existence and loneliness, that's where I see you, meet you; in your struggle to live, I will give to help you live.

LONDON

I see you close, almost feel your pain, could easily feed your hunger, know your sorrow, and search for a tomorrow.

The single cost of just one of the lenses in my camera would keep you alive for a month. It's relative but it makes no sense, I am the reporter of your every breath, shallow and weak as it is, as that may be, ignore me now while I take your plight across the wires to those who sit in front of fires.

ESSEX

I see your face, your eyes plead with my soul, crying out from the shiny pages of the magazine that I subscribe to on a monthly basis, to read while I eat the best food and wine that money can buy, as my working week in the city is over, when I am quite sure I deserve this treat, but you!

Your treat is just water, clean fresh water that's all.

I will give and give and give, I want you to live, to be healthy happy and free to play and survive.

FRANCE

The factory where I work produces the best food, food that will keep you and those like you alive, made from peanut paste, vegetable oil, powdered milk, powdered sugar, vitamins, and minerals, it's to keep those like you alive, we work, we work and we send it to investors in you and those like you - therapeutic food they call it with 2,100 calories per packet.

We make, you take and you will live.... dear sweet child of this human race, you will live...we will give....

Sue Daniels has written and published series of Self Help Booklets appropriate to the work that she does. Her passion though, is humanitarian poetry and extrasensory fiction. Whatever she writes, it is always, sourced from the heart.

The Hall of Empty

by Leonie Spence

I was given a pass
Into the hall of emptiness,
Was told to fill it
While I was there,
As I gazed around the unkept barren walls,
I wondered how did she get that way?
Surely she was fulfilled
What was hanging on these walls?
Who had danced singed loved with all their heart?
Did these things exist before?
I remember now
The dance ended long ago,
Replaced by life's demands
The singing I hear her echo,
Now only the voice of order and combat,
The ache can still be felt
They cry,
Oh how they cry
Free this soul of dance
The one who would dare,
These walls became full of decaying things
Poisons of the soul,
And now alone I stand in the hall of emptiness.

I am 30 years of age and currently reside in the north of England . I have been an avid reader of spiritual text for the last 15 years, my main interest being finding ones path to the authentic within, and loosing ego's grip, through the practice of meditation. I also have a great interest in holistic healing modalities and have been a reiki and angelic reiki practitioner for the last four years. I feel a calling to write and share my works, which I hope will help or inspire in some way.

@lilmissholistic (Instagram)   *leoniespence@googlemail.com*

A Horse called Blessing

By Barbara Collins

It's never too late to find your heart's desire,
although she tried as a child, a hose she never acquired.
"Wait until we find the perfect one,"
she was told, but that day would never come.
So in the country she made her home,
on enough land that she and her dog could roam.
Her life has had its ups and downs,
and at times she just wanted to leave this town.
The Maine coast pulled her away a few times,
she'd walk the rocky shoreline thinking of all the
responsibilities she'd left behind.
"My children are my pride and joy" she'd say,
"They help me make it through each day."
Divine timing is certainly an amazing thing,
for when the right moment comes,
a blessing it can bring.
And with the loss of her son she did find,
a love of a very unexpected kind.
A beautiful horse that suffered from human neglect,
now rescued, it grazed in the field near her homestead.
One day he found a weak spot in the fence,
and across the road to her home he fled.
Seeing him out and running free,

she said to him, "Be a good pony and come to me."
Now grabbing his bridle and walking him home,
so began the bond of woman and foal.
Her days were spent like a cowboy she corralled,

bringing him back to his field while taking the long way
around.
A friendship born of trust,
soon turned to respect and love.
This horse called Blessing was sent to heal,
with a little help from above.

I'm a stay-at-home mom who works online as a life coach and spiritual guide. I write to express my creative side and also as a tool in healing the soul. Most of my writing is poetry, short stories and erotica. This poem is about an actual experience my mother had while grieving the loss of my brother's death, so I gifted her this poem.

Shore

by Cheryl Secomb

On the day we buried Samuel,
I found a small smooth stone,
sitting alone on the shore.

I rolled it over and over in my palm.
Touching its calm,
cool surface soothed me.

How long had it tumbled,
searching for shore?
Tossed,
swirling, whirling
dipping, whipping.

Like me,
drowning.

But there it sat,
resting on the beach,
out of reach,
safe from the waves.

I slipped the small stone
into my pocket
to remind me

there's a shore.

I enjoy writing fiction for children. I've had stories published in Clubhouse Jr. magazine, LIVE publication, and several anthologies. I believe that poetry teaches a writer to add beauty to her writing and I recently took a class taught by Renee LaTulippe called The Lyrical Language Lab. The poem here was written as an assignment during this class with the idea of it being part of a novel in verse. Now I just have to write the novel!

I'm a member of Oregon Christian Writers and live in Oregon with my husband, four grown children and five grandchildren. I like reading, writing and spending time with my family. Thank you for taking the time to read my poem.

Surrender

by Aleshia Priester Howell

I felt it encasing me...
raptured in this feeling...
bliss...elation...
tranquility...
What a sensation...
not like any I'd ever known...
this love...so delightful I'd experienced
stirred me to tears.
His Love...pure...irreplaceable...unmeasurable...
erasing all fears...
A Love of One Who loves me better...
than anyone could...ever...

...love me enough to say "Father forgive her
allow me to take blame for that sin...
allow me to carry that burden.
I will wait for her to release all of the hurt,
the sorrows and heartaches...
Maybe today will be the day she surrenders...
What will it take...to have her relinquish this
battle to me...
realizing it never was hers...
for I've already won that victory?"

I, take heed of His whispers
as he sits on the throne
interceding for me...
as I walked paths not created for me...
spouted words unbecoming of me...
hated when I should have loved...
without condition...
found it difficult to forgive...

even though I'd been forgiven.

I find myself in this place of worship…so sweet
ushered into His presence…
I bow head and knee in reverence
and I whisper...
ALL TO THEE...
I SURRENDER...

Hello, I'm Aleshia Priester Howell also known as Mz. Poetic Flow…Savannah Georgia born and Jacksonville North Carolina reared. I'm a single mother of four…an English major in college focusing on Creative Writing. As a young girl I realized I had a love for writing and recognized poetry as a passion a few years ago and began hosting poetry events in my town to showcase local poets and to enlighten others to the beauty and wonder that is "Poetry". Within me lies a strong desire to bring joy and encouragement to the world through my poetic flow. As God whispers, I will birth the rhythmic utterance.

Experience Brain Injury

by Carol Nickerson-Goguen

Many thoughts running through this brain
Knows that spirit is one in the same
A fall on the head let me know for sure
The pain that it left I cannot endure

Memories of life this spirit subsist
Now not to experience a morsel of bliss
Existence in this body clouded in haze
Negative objects take front stage

Have come to realize the weight of body
The consumption used leaves me melancholy
To continue the drugs Doctors prescribe
Makes this persona want to cry

It's hard to remain within this realm
Abandonment of loved ones is overwhelm
It wasn't this body's time to leave this earth
The experience gained expelled the mirth

A Home

by Shiner Day

Sometimes, especially after having moved a great deal,
we get tired and settle down in the first available rental.
It is really cramped and there are already a lot of things
out,
not really leaving any room for your baggage.
The place is relatively cold, drafty, and not particularly
safe.
The majority of the main, vital, essential, crucial, and all
around imperative
fixtures are broken.
None the matter how hard you try to fix them and get
them working right again.
All your efforts are in vain,
leaving you with bruised hands from trying to tighten the
bolts to hold this house together.
Despite these many inconveniences,
you still unpack.
You pull out your most precious things,
your most beautiful possessions.
You place them all around this house hoping to bring it to
life
and add some color and light
to this crumbling mass.
One day,
the house gives on itself with you still inside.
One of several faulty wires,
that you were planning to address later,
has sprung free and the house starts to burn.
In this moment,
it occurs to you to wonder why you hadn't left sooner,
why you stayed
when the floor board gave way beneath your weight,
why you stayed

when you had to sit in solid, thick, suffocating darkness
because the lights wouldn't come on,
why you stayed
that cold time when the heater wouldn't fully wake to keep
you warm like it should,
but instead just blew cool unpleasantness at you
as if that were some sort of worthy substitute.
All aside,
you wanted to save this house,
all aside,
you convinced yourself that you actually could.
But more than anything,
you just didn't want to be homeless,
out there,
alone,
just searching aimlessly
again.
And you know now
why you saw the cracks in the walls,
lurid as they were,
and just reassured yourself that it simply gave this place
character.
You just thought these defects could be gone back over
later.
Fixed.
Eventually.
Now you have to make a choice.
The choice.
This house has turned on itself regardless of you.
You can stay,
burn with it,
or
you can run
and try to salvage your things,
your beloved belongings.
So,
in this moment, you realize you haven't had a home

before.
You want one.
Deserve one, even.
So, you run.
You gather your things, your wonderful things that haven't
been burned or broken yet.
You throw yourself from the house, rescues in hand.
Running as fast as you can, you feel the weight of the
treasures the house stole from you,
how you wish you had just left while all of your luggage
was still intact,
if you just hadn't unpacked...
Reaching the hill, overlooking the house you wanted so
badly,
the house gives one last cry then caves in completely.
It is only now that you see what the house had been
harboring,
a deep, dark basement,
the room you always knew was there, but chose to pretend
it was something else.
Something cleaner.
Not a basement, just a closet maybe.
The room you were never able to enter
because the door wouldn't budge,
is now gaping open for all,
and it took the house falling apart for it to be exposed.
The flames of the still burning house light the rot
and years of dust and dirt in the space the house held
below.
It would appear that no light has been shed or
maintenance made to this secret room.
Not for a long time.
Untouched.
Fragile.
You witness all of the house's own photographs and
stored suitcases burn;
all these things you never knew the house held

because it never let you in.
Not this room.
The door to this hold would never open for you,
probably not for anyone.
Maybe this is why your foot had gone through the floor.
The core was too weak to withstand you.
Not strong enough for you.
As you watch the ashes of the lost hope rise,
you feel the Sun on your back.
Bright.
Warm.
He is there.
Your heart lightens as He bears the burden with you,
for you.
"Dad,
I really loved that house."
"Child,
that's not the one I built for you."
Glancing down at the remaining things in your arms,
your heart tightens with loss.
Grief.
"I lost so much. I couldn't save it all. These are the only
things left."
"Treasured,
I can replace what you lost. These things are already paid for,
if you will accept them."
"What if they aren't like the ones I had?"
"Beloved,
I assure you, I replace your glass with diamond.
Follow me now.
Let me take you home."
The unknown is unwelcome,
but the maker of the beginning and the end
is safe.
To decide to follow the one who knows what lies at the
end of the road,
is to have a home.

I was born January 20, 1994. It wasn't until the freshly turned age of 21 that I discovered, unfortunately, I was a writer. I had had other plans for myself that involved being more neutral and less bolding opinionated. However, I gladly accept such a beautiful talent over none. I confirmed my tendency to jot thought once I fully acknowledged how many pencils had gone missing in my hair. I truly hope my work is as enjoyed being read and it is being wrote.

You Make My Heart Smile

by Robyn Campbell

You are a symphony in
my heart.

A sweet-sounding orchestra
songful, honeyed, pleasing to
my soul.

Others look at your face and
gawk at the wine colored
birthmark.

Goggling, ogling as if you were
a freak.

The silence makes you feel so
alone.

Like a single mockingbird;
empty.

You seem lost in the shadows
of life.

Grieving for normalcy and
consent.

Why can't the world see you as
I do?

Why is the world embarrassed by
your face?

How can human be so
vicious?

Why are civilized people so
callous?

When will the hurt wash away from
your eyes?

You whisper, why are they
staring.

In hushed tones, you speak of your
feelings.

Yes, you hurt like all human
beings.

Do they believe you're
a rock?

Unable to sense the vibes they
diffuse?

How many times will I watch
you cry?

How many tears will my heart bleed
for you?

Sickened because the world looks
through you.

Instead of looking
at you.

But then you give me that handsome

peering into the heart of
God smile.

The grin that rains pure joy on
my day.

Then I weep; for the world can't
fathom
what they miss in not knowing
my son.

Written for my son Christopher and to everyone born with
Sturge-Weber Syndrome.

*Robyn Campbell is a children's writer and poet who lives on a farm
in NC. When not homeschooling and riding one of her horses, she
writes in the barn with all the sounds of nature.*

How People Make Me Feel

by Ibrahim Dosso

People are strange creatures

They are mysterious one minute

Then an open book the next minute

People don't come with warnings or knowledge

People are just outrageous objects of earth's creation

People confuse me

They have such a dynamic range of emotions

They can be happy, smart, generous humans

The can turn into evil, disrespectful, stupid, lazy animals

People don't know how their flaws and perfections can
affect others

People disappoint me

They can lie, steal, cheat, and kill like it doesn't matter

They can be sweet and generous when they want to be

And be distant, cold, and miscalculating without thought

People's actions always leave me in a state of disarray

People interest me

Learning people's personal lives is a fetish of mine

I enjoy seeing and reading what people do outside the

public eye

Seeing one's personality traits and characteristics is my aphrodisiac

People's lives are always someone else's fascination

People entice me

People's likes and dislikes are something that gives me rampant thoughts

What people find beautiful and sexy is so exciting to find out

Every human is different and had unique philosophies

How a human feels is the precious thing in the universe

People comfort me

We all have little things we have flaws

To see someone else in a state of disillusionment is illuminating

Everyone is perfectly imperfect and no one is perfect

We are all different and lead different lives

People are amazing

What Do You Live For?

by Lily Shaver

I was talking with this kid today
He asked me a question
That really got me to thinkin'
"What do you live for" he asked
"What keeps you goin'"
I pondered this a while
Then I began to smile and said
The sun and the sky
The leaves on the trees
The cool evening breeze
God grant that I live on my knees
And never forget what I live for
A newborn baby's cry
A mother's calming lullaby
Even roaring thunder
Bursts of lightning
God created all of these
Mountains so lofty
Valleys low
Oceans vast
I live to proclaim
The glory
Of the one who created
The very world I live in

Lily Shaver is an aspiring journalist and writer.

In Closing...

We hope you have enjoyed our 2015 poetry anthology, *Illuminations of the Soul*. If you were touched by a certain poem, or perhaps by the collection as a whole, please do these poets a service and pay it forward by spreading the word with your friends, family and within your community.

If you enjoyed this collection and would like to further help support this project, we ask you to please consider taking a moment to write a review on Amazon.com. Your time and effort to leave a positive review will support the efforts of the artists within these pages, whose talents deserve to be seen and shared with the world.

For more daily inspiration, please visit us at www.spiritualwritersnetwork.com. There is something for everyone at Spiritual Writers Network, and it's free to register, write and share on our network. Stay tuned for upcoming writing contests as well.

Perhaps *YOU* will be the next author chosen for publication!

Other Collections
by Spiritual Writers Network

Love & Light: A Collection of Inspirational Stories and Poems

Reflections of the Soul: 2013 Poetry Anthology

Touched by an Angel: A Collection of Divinely Inspired Stories & Poems

The Best of Spiritual Writers Network 2013

Whispers of the Soul: A Poetry Anthology

The Best of Spiritual Writers Network 2014

Website:
www.SpiritualWritersNetwork.com

Facebook:
www.Facebook.com/spiritualwritersnetwork

Twitter:
www.Twitter.com/swn444

Printed in Great Britain
by Amazon